SCHOLASTIC

Do The Math™

Created by **Marilyn Burns**

Division C

Dividends to 1,000

WorkSpace

Credits: cover: © David Madison/Getty Images; pp. 19; 20; 22; 24–25; 27–35: Frank Montagna © Scholastic Inc.

Published by Scholastic Inc. Printed in the U.S.A.

ISBN-13: 978-0-545-02260-6
ISBN-10: 0-545-02260-6

9 10 40 16 15 14

v.B

The 25th Squadron

DIRECTIONS

groups of 6

1

$25 \div 6 = 4 \text{ R}1$

Write a division equation.

2

Can Joe march with the 25th squadron in groups of 6? no

Answer the question.

3

dividend 25
divisor 6
quotient 4
remainder 1

Fill in the blanks.

25th squadron

1 groups of 7

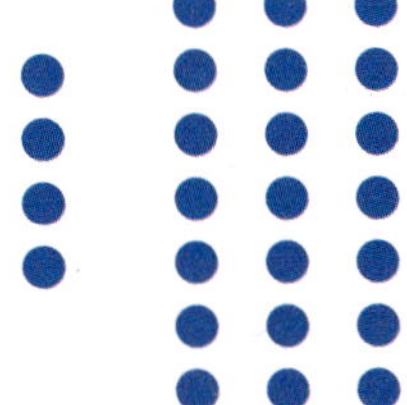

dividend ______
divisor ______
quotient ______
remainder ______

Equation: ____________________

Can Joe march with the 25th squadron when it marches in groups of 7? ______

2 groups of 8

dividend ______
divisor ______
quotient ______
remainder ______

Equation: ____________________

Can Joe march with the 25th squadron when it marches in groups of 8? ______

3 groups of 9

dividend ______
divisor ______
quotient ______
remainder ______

Equation: ____________________

Can Joe march with the 25th squadron when it marches in groups of 9? ______

4 groups of 10

dividend ______
divisor ______
quotient ______
remainder ______

Equation: ____________________

Can Joe march with the 25th squadron when it marches in groups of 10? ______

Home Note: Your child writes division equations to solve problems.

The 24th Squadron

DIRECTIONS

groups of 2

$24 \div 2 =$ ____

1

$12 \times 2 = 24$

Write a multiplication equation.

2

$24 \div 2 =$ 12

Fill in the answer.

3

Is 24 divisible by 2? yes

Answer the question.

24th squadron

1. **groups of 2**

   $24 \div 2 =$ ____

   Is 24 divisible by 2? ____

2. **groups of 3**

   $24 \div 3 =$ ____

   Is 24 divisible by 3? ____

3. **groups of 4**

   $24 \div 4 =$ ____

   Is 24 divisible by 4? ____

4. **groups of 5**

   $24 \div 5 =$ ____

   Is 24 divisible by 5? ____

Home Note: Your child writes multiplication and division equations to solve problems.

The 30th Squadron

DIRECTIONS

groups of 2

$30 \div 2 =$ ____

1

$15 \times 2 = 30$

Write a multiplication equation.

2

$30 \div 2 =$ 15

Fill in the answer.

3

Is 30 divisible by 2? yes

Answer the question.

30th squadron

1. groups of 2

   $30 \div 2 =$ ____

   Is 30 divisible by 2? ____

2. groups of 3

   $30 \div 3 =$ ____

   Is 30 divisible by 3? ____

3. groups of 4

   $30 \div 4 =$ ____

   Is 30 divisible by 4? ____

4. groups of 5

   $30 \div 5 =$ ____

   Is 30 divisible by 5? ____

Home Note: Your child writes multiplication and division equations to solve problems.

The 32nd Squadron

DIRECTIONS

groups of 2

32 ÷ 2 = ____

1

16 × 2 = 32

Write a multiplication equation.

2

32 ÷ 2 = 16

Fill in the answer.

3

Is 32 divisible by 2? yes

Answer the question.

32nd squadron

① **groups of 2**

32 ÷ 2 = ____

Is 32 divisible by 2? ____

② **groups of 3**

32 ÷ 3 = ____

Is 32 divisible by 3? ____

③ **groups of 4**

32 ÷ 4 = ____

Is 32 divisible by 4? ____

④ **groups of 5**

32 ÷ 5 = ____

Is 32 divisible by 5? ____

Home Note: Your child writes multiplication and division equations to solve problems.

The 20th Squadron

DIRECTIONS

groups of 2

$20 \div 2 =$ ____

1

$10 \times 2 = 20$

Write a multiplication equation.

2

$20 \div 2 =$ 10

Fill in the answer.

3

Is 20 divisible by 2? yes

Answer the question.

20th squadron

1. **groups of 2**

   $20 \div 2 =$ ____

   Is 20 divisible by 2? ____

2. **groups of 3**

   $20 \div 3 =$ ____

   Is 20 divisible by 3? ____

3. **groups of 4**

   $20 \div 4 =$ ____

   Is 20 divisible by 4? ____

4. **groups of 5**

   $20 \div 5 =$ ____

   Is 20 divisible by 5? ____

Home Note: Your child writes multiplication and division equations to solve problems.

The 40th Squadron

DIRECTIONS

groups of 2

$40 \div 2 =$ ____

1

$20 \times 2 = 40$

Write a multiplication equation.

2

$40 \div 2 =$ 20

Fill in the answer.

3

Is 40 divisible by 2? yes

Answer the question.

40th squadron

1. **groups of 2**

   $40 \div 2 =$ ____

   Is 40 divisible by 2? ____

2. **groups of 3**

   $40 \div 3 =$ ____

   Is 40 divisible by 3? ____

3. **groups of 4**

   $40 \div 4 =$ ____

   Is 40 divisible by 4? ____

4. **groups of 5**

   $40 \div 5 =$ ____

   Is 40 divisible by 5? ____

Home Note: Your child writes multiplication and division equations to solve problems.

Rules for Target 1000

HOW TO PLAY

What you need

- red number cube (1–6)
- *WorkSpace* page 9

➤ **A game is six turns for each player.**

➤ **Players add their answers from each turn to their previous scores.**

1

Player A rolls the number cube.

2

10 20 30 40 ~~50~~ 60 70 80 90 100

$4 \times \underline{50} = 200$

Player A multiplies the number on the cube by one of the tens numbers and then crosses out the tens number.

3

Player A hands the cube to Player B.

4

10 20 30 40 50 ~~60~~ 70 80 90 100

$5 \times \underline{60} = 300$

Player B takes a turn.

➤ **The winner is the player whose score is closer to 1000—without going over—after six turns.**

Home Note: Your child practices multiplying by multiples of 10 while playing a game.

Target 1000

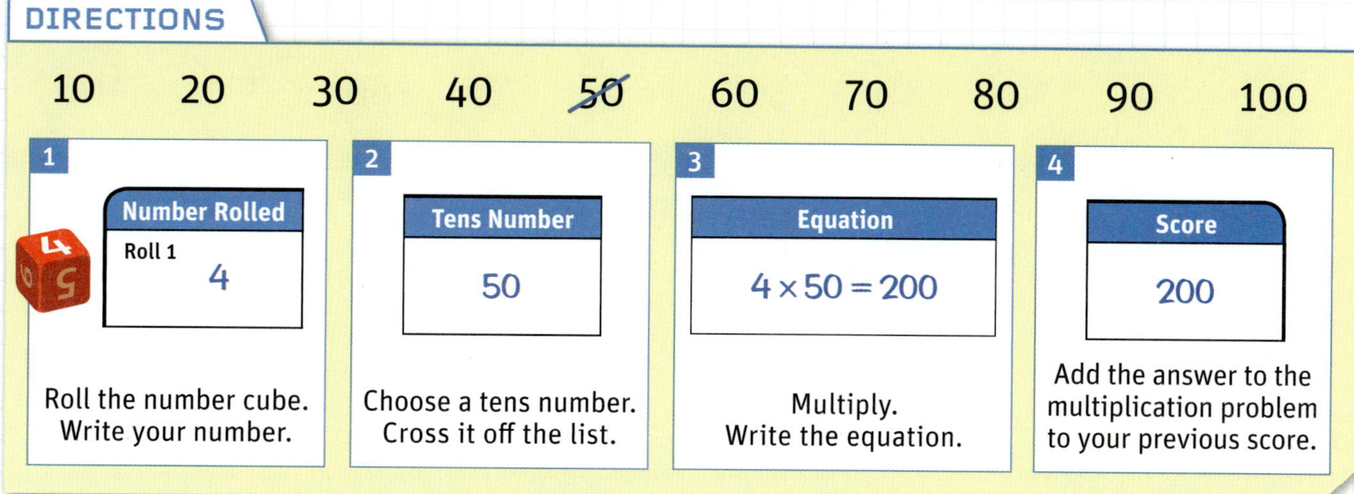

10 20 30 40 50 60 70 80 90 100

Number Rolled	Tens Number	Equation	Score
Roll 1			
Roll 2			
Roll 3			
Roll 4			
Roll 5			
Roll 6			TOTAL

Home Note: Your child practices multiplying by multiples of 10 while playing a game.

Target 1000

DIRECTIONS

10 20 30 40 ~~50~~ 60 70 80 90 100

1	2	3	4
Number Rolled Roll 1: 4	Tens Number 50	Equation $4 \times 50 = 200$	Score 200
Roll the number cube. Write your number.	Choose a tens number. Cross it off the list.	Multiply. Write the equation.	Add the answer to the multiplication problem to your previous score.

10 20 30 40 50 60 70 80 90 100

Number Rolled	Tens Number	Equation	Score
Roll 1			
Roll 2			
Roll 3			
Roll 4			
Roll 5			
Roll 6			
			TOTAL

Home Note: Your child practices multiplying by multiples of 10 while playing a game.

Show What You Know

DIRECTIONS

- Write a multiplication equation.
- Write the answer to the division problem.
- Answer the question.

18th squadron

① groups of 2	② groups of 3
$18 \div 2 =$ _____ Is 18 divisible by 2? _____	$18 \div 3 =$ _____ Is 18 divisible by 3? _____
③ **groups of 4** $18 \div 4 =$ _____ Is 18 divisible by 4? _____	④ **groups of 5** $18 \div 5 =$ _____ Is 18 divisible by 5? _____

Home Note: Your child writes multiplication and division equations to solve problems.

Show What You Know

DIRECTIONS

➤ Write the answer for each equation.

① 5 × 60 = ______	② 2 × 100 = ______
③ 3 × 20 = ______	④ 6 × 80 = ______
⑤ 4 × 90 = ______	⑥ 1 × 40 = ______
⑦ 5 × 70 = ______	⑧ 6 × 70 = ______

➤ Fill in the blanks.

⑨ 25 ÷ 8 = 3 R1 dividend ______ divisor ______ quotient ______ remainder ______	⑩ 16 ÷ 3 = 5 R1 dividend ______ divisor ______ quotient ______ remainder ______

Home Note: Your child multiplies by multiples of 10 and divides by one-digit numbers.

Target 1000

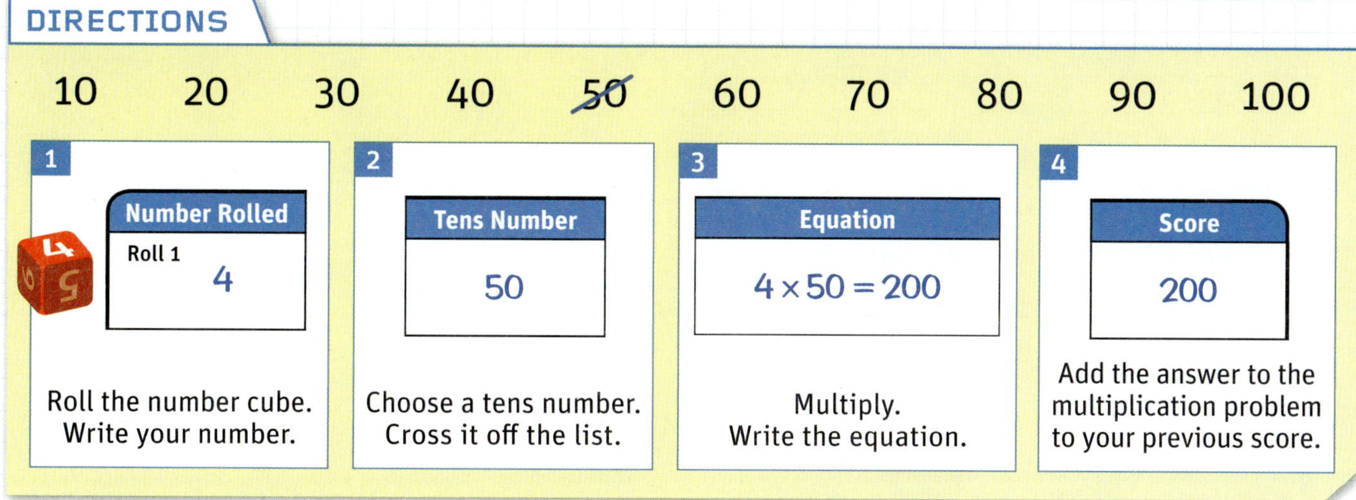

10 20 30 40 50 60 70 80 90 100

Number Rolled	Tens Number	Equation	Score
Roll 1			
Roll 2			
Roll 3			
Roll 4			
Roll 5			
Roll 6			TOTAL

Home Note: Your child practices multiplying by multiples of 10 while playing a game.

Rules for Target Zero

HOW TO PLAY

What you need

- red number cube (1–6)
- *WorkSpace* page 15

➤ **A game is six turns for each player.**

➤ **Players start with a score of 1000. They subtract their amounts from each turn from their previous scores.**

1

Player A rolls the number cube.

2

10 20 30 40 50 60 70 80 90 ~~100~~

$1000 - 200 = 800$

Player A multiplies the number on the cube by one of the tens numbers, crosses out the tens number, and subtracts his or her score from 1000.

3

Player A hands the cube to Player B.

4

10 20 30 40 50 60 70 ~~80~~ 90 100

$3 \times \underline{80} = 240$

$1000 - 240 = 760$

Player B takes a turn.

➤ **The winner is the player whose score is closer to 0—without going under—after six turns.**

Home Note: Your child practices subtracting by playing a game.

Target Zero

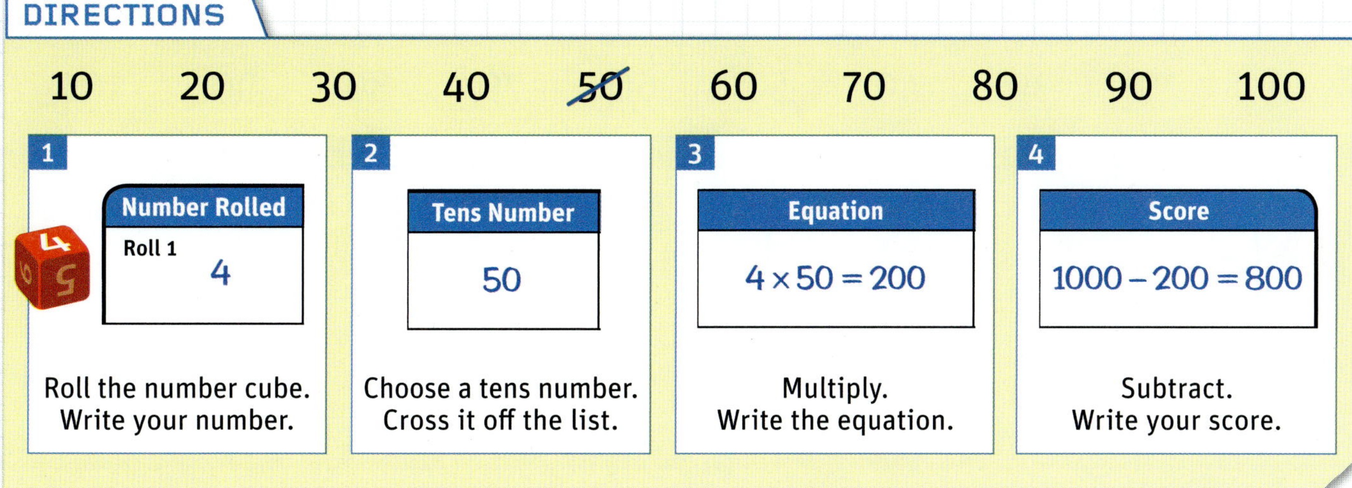

10 20 30 40 50 60 70 80 90 100

Number Rolled	Tens Number	Equation	Score
Roll 1			
Roll 2			
Roll 3			
Roll 4			
Roll 5			
Roll 6			TOTAL

Home Note: Your child practices subtracting while playing a game.

Target Zero

DIRECTIONS

10 20 30 40 ~~50~~ 60 70 80 90 100

1. **Number Rolled** — Roll 1: 4
Roll the number cube. Write your number.

2. **Tens Number** — 50
Choose a tens number. Cross it off the list.

3. **Equation** — $4 \times 50 = 200$
Multiply. Write the equation.

4. **Score** — $1000 - 200 = 800$
Subtract. Write your score.

10 20 30 40 50 60 70 80 90 100

Number Rolled	Tens Number	Equation	Score
Roll 1			
Roll 2			
Roll 3			
Roll 4			
Roll 5			
Roll 6			TOTAL

Home Note: Your child practices subtracting while playing a game.

Target Zero

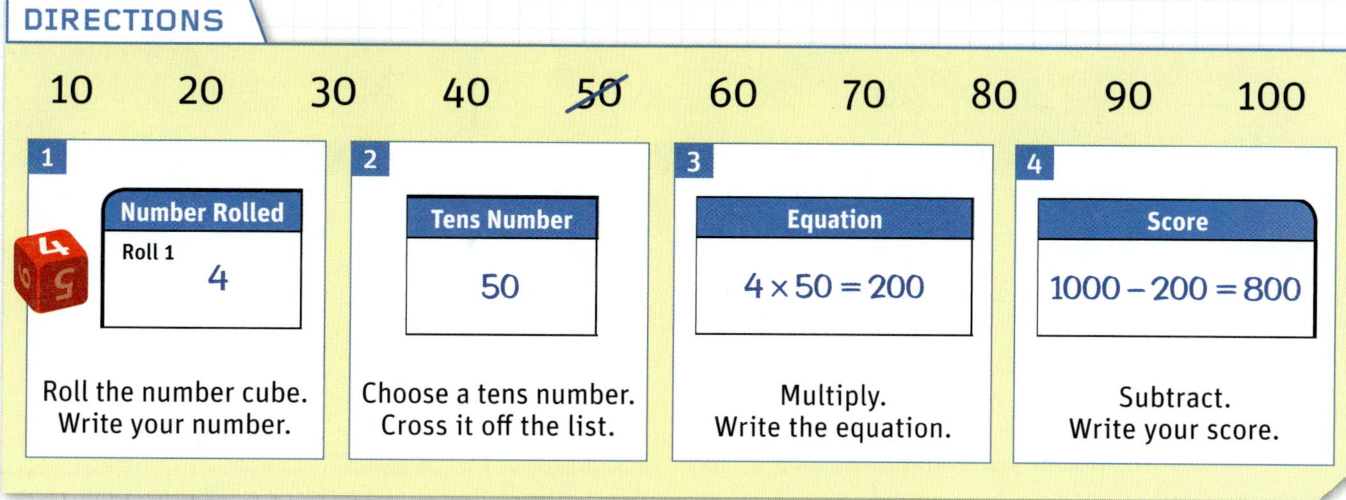

10 20 30 40 50 60 70 80 90 100

Number Rolled	Tens Number	Equation	Score
Roll 1			
Roll 2			
Roll 3			
Roll 4			
Roll 5			
Roll 6			TOTAL

Home Note: Your child practices subtracting while playing a game.

Target Zero

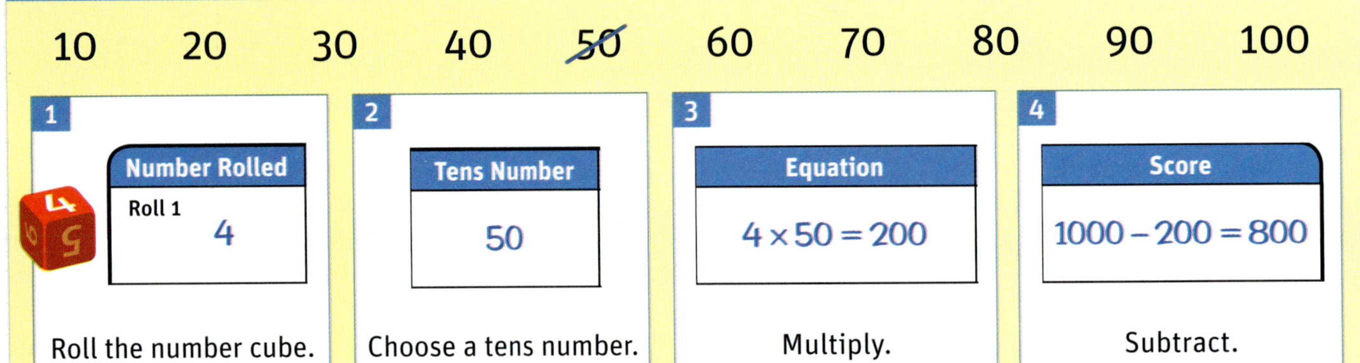

10 20 30 40 50 60 70 80 90 100

Number Rolled	Tens Number	Equation	Score
Roll 1			
Roll 2			
Roll 3			
Roll 4			
Roll 5			
Roll 6			TOTAL

Home Note: Your child practices subtracting while playing a game.

A Tricycle Problem

DIRECTIONS

Louie brings 17 wheels.

How many tricycles can be put together? ______

How many wheels will be left over? ______

1	2	3	4
$3\overline{)17}$	5 R2 $3\overline{)17}$ $\underline{15}$ ⑤ $\times 3 = 15$ 2	$5 \times 3 = 15$ $15 + 2 = 17$	How many tricycles can be put together? 5 How many wheels will be left over? 2
Write the division problem.	Solve the division problem.	Check your answer.	Answer the questions.

Louie brings 27 wheels.

How many tricycles can be put together? ______

How many wheels will be left over? ______

Work Area

Home Note: Your child solves problems with the divisor 3.

Tricycle Problems

DIRECTIONS

Louie brings 17 wheels.

How many tricycles can be put together? ____

How many wheels will be left over? ____

1

$$3\overline{)17} \quad 5\ R2$$
$$15 \quad ⑤ \times 3 = 15$$
$$2$$

Write the division problem and solve it.

2

$5 \times 3 = 15$

$15 + 2 = 17$

Check your answer.

3

How many tricycles can be put together? 5

How many wheels will be left over? 2

Answer the questions.

Problem	Solve	Check
① Louie brings 19 wheels. How many tricycles can be put together? ____ How many wheels will be left over? ____		
② Louie brings 20 wheels. How many tricycles can be put together? ____ How many wheels will be left over? ____		

Home Note: Your child solves problems with the divisor 3.

Target Zero

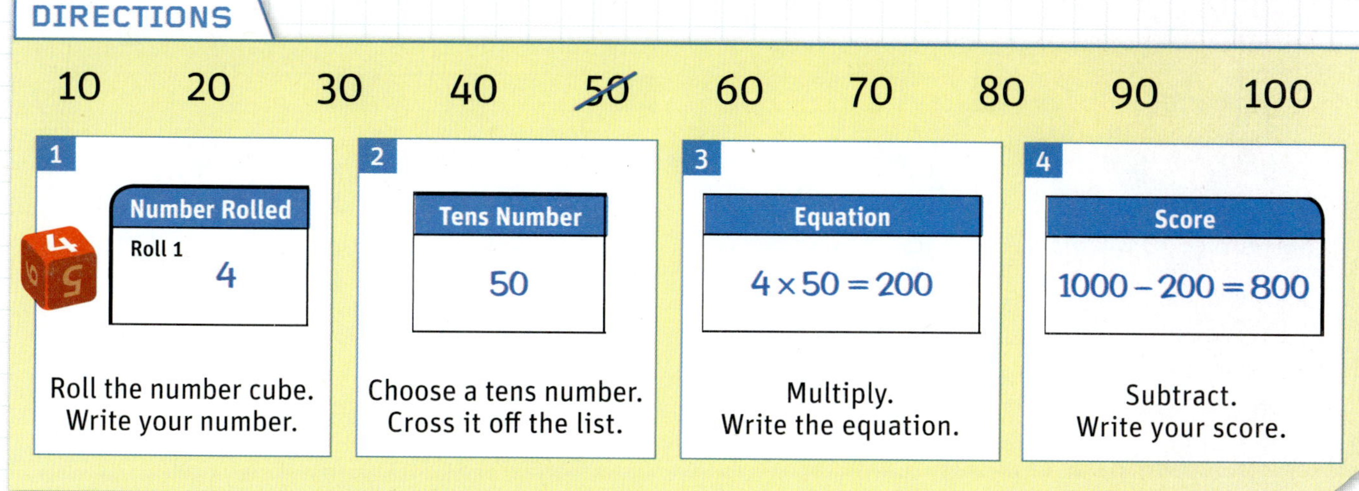

10 20 30 40 50 60 70 80 90 100

Number Rolled	Tens Number	Equation	Score
Roll 1			
Roll 2			
Roll 3			
Roll 4			
Roll 5			
Roll 6			TOTAL

Home Note: Your child practices subtracting while playing a game.

Toy Car Problems

DIRECTIONS

Louie brings 30 wheels.

How many toy cars can be put together? ______

How many wheels will be left over? ______

1

$$\begin{array}{r} 7\text{ R}2 \\ 4\overline{)30} \\ \underline{28} \\ 2 \end{array} \qquad ⑦ \times 4 = 28$$

Write the division problem and solve it.

2

$7 \times 4 = 28$

$28 + 2 = 30$

Check your answer.

3

How many toy cars can be put together? 7

How many wheels will be left over? 2

Answer the questions.

Problem	Solve	Check
(1) Louie brings 35 wheels. How many toy cars can be put together? ______ How many wheels will be left over? ______		
(2) Louie brings 36 wheels. How many toy cars can be put together? ______ How many wheels will be left over? ______		
(3) Louie brings 29 wheels. How many toy cars can be put together? ______ How many wheels will be left over? ______		

Home Note: Your child solves problems with the divisor 4.

Target Zero

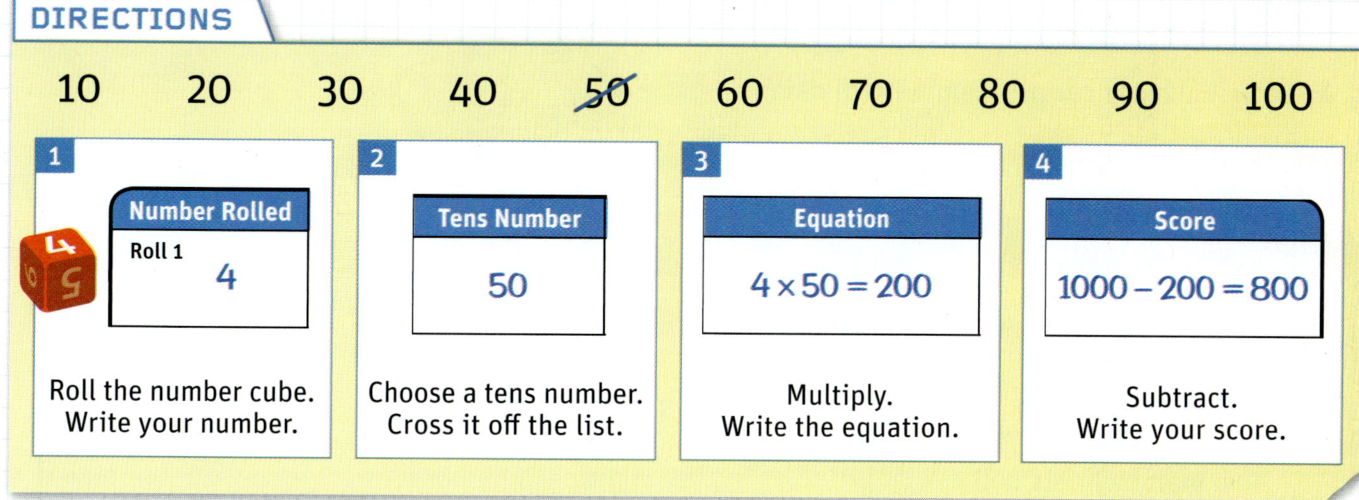

10 20 30 40 50 60 70 80 90 100

Number Rolled	Tens Number	Equation	Score
Roll 1			
Roll 2			
Roll 3			
Roll 4			
Roll 5			
Roll 6			TOTAL

Home Note: Your child practices subtracting while playing a game.

Show What You Know

DIRECTIONS

➤ Solve each toy car problem with division.

Problem	Solve	Check
(1) Louie brings 39 wheels. How many toy cars can be put together? _____ How many wheels will be left over? _____		
(2) Louie brings 22 wheels. How many toy cars can be put together? _____ How many wheels will be left over? _____		
(3) Louie brings 27 wheels. How many toy cars can be put together? _____ How many wheels will be left over? _____		

Home Note: Your child solves problems with the divisor 4.

Show What You Know

DIRECTIONS

➤ Solve each tricycle problem with division.

Problem	Solve	Check
(1) Louie brings 29 wheels. How many tricycles can be put together? ______ How many wheels will be left over? ______		
(2) Louie brings 22 wheels. How many tricycles can be put together? ______ How many wheels will be left over? ______		
(3) Louie brings 18 wheels. How many tricycles can be put together? ______ How many wheels will be left over? ______		

Home Note: Your child solves problems with the divisor 3.

Target Zero

DIRECTIONS

10 20 30 40 ~~50~~ 60 70 80 90 100

1 **Number Rolled**
Roll 1 4

Roll the number cube.
Write your number.

2 **Tens Number**
50

Choose a tens number.
Cross it off the list.

3 **Equation**
$4 \times 50 = 200$

Multiply.
Write the equation.

4 **Score**
$1000 - 200 = 800$

Subtract.
Write your score.

10 20 30 40 50 60 70 80 90 100

Number Rolled	Tens Number	Equation	Score
Roll 1			
Roll 2			
Roll 3			
Roll 4			
Roll 5			
Roll 6			TOTAL

Home Note: Your child practices subtracting while playing a game.

Tricycle Problems

DIRECTIONS

Louie brings 43 wheels.

How many tricycles can we put together? _____

How many wheels will be left over? _____

1

$$3\overline{)43}$$

4		14 R1
10		
3)43		
30	(10) × 3 = 30	
13		
12	(4) × 3 = 12	
1		

Write the division problem and solve it.

2

$14 \times 3 = 42$

$42 + 1 = 43$

Check your answer.

3

How many tricycles can we put together? 14

How many wheels will be left over? 1

Answer the questions.

Problem	Solve	Check
(1) Louie brings 34 wheels. How many tricycles can we put together? _____ How many wheels will be left over? _____		
(2) Louie brings 49 wheels. How many tricycles can we put together? _____ How many wheels will be left over? _____		
(3) Louie brings 45 wheels. How many tricycles can we put together? _____ How many wheels will be left over? _____		

Home Note: Your child solves problems with the divisor 3.

Tricycle Problems

DIRECTIONS

Louie brings 74 wheels.

How many tricycles can we put together? ______

How many wheels will be left over? ______

1

$$\begin{array}{r} 4 \\ 10 \\ 10 \\ 3\overline{)74} \\ \underline{30} \\ 44 \\ \underline{30} \\ 14 \\ \underline{12} \\ 2 \end{array}$$

24 R2

(10) × 3 = 30

(10) × 3 = 30

(4) × 3 = 12

Write the division problem and solve it.

2

$24 \times 3 = 72$

$72 + 2 = 74$

Check your answer.

3

How many tricycles can we put together? 24

How many wheels will be left over? 2

Answer the questions.

Problem	Solve	Check
(1) Louie brings 81 wheels. How many tricycles can we put together? ______ How many wheels will be left over? ______		

Home Note: Your child solves problems with the divisor 3.

Tricycle Problems

DIRECTIONS

Louie brings 74 wheels.

How many tricycles can we put together? ______

How many wheels will be left over? ______

1

$$\begin{array}{r} 4 \\ 10 \\ 10 \\ 3\overline{)74} \\ \underline{30} \\ 44 \\ \underline{30} \\ 14 \\ \underline{12} \\ 2 \end{array}$$

4 + 10 + 10 → 24 R2

⑩ × 3 = 30

⑩ × 3 = 30

④ × 3 = 12

Write the division problem and solve it.

2

$24 \times 3 = 72$

$72 + 2 = 74$

Check your answer.

3

How many tricycles can we put together? 24

How many wheels will be left over? 2

Answer the questions.

Problem	Solve	Check
(1) Louie brings 79 wheels. How many tricycles can we put together? ______ How many wheels will be left over? ______		
(2) Louie brings 73 wheels. How many tricycles can we put together? ______ How many wheels will be left over? ______		

Home Note: Your child solves problems with the divisor 3.

Toy Car Problems

DIRECTIONS

Louie brings 83 wheels.

How many toy cars can we put together? ______

How many wheels will be left over? ______

1

10	
10	→ 20 R3
4)83	
40	⑩ $\times 4 = 40$
43	
40	⑩ $\times 4 = 40$
3	

Write the division problem and solve it.

2

$20 \times 4 = 80$

$80 + 3 = 83$

Check your answer.

3

How many toy cars can we put together? 20

How many wheels will be left over? 3

Answer the question.

Problem	Solve	Check
(1) Louie brings 98 wheels. How many toy cars can we put together? ______ How many wheels will be left over? ______		

Home Note: Your child solves problems with the divisor 4.

Toy Car Problems

DIRECTIONS

Louie brings 83 wheels.

How many toy cars can we put together? ______

How many wheels will be left over? ______

1

$$
\begin{array}{r}
10 \\
10 \\
4\overline{)83} \\
40 \\
43 \\
40 \\
3
\end{array}
\quad \text{20 R3} \qquad \textcircled{10} \times 4 = 40 \qquad \textcircled{10} \times 4 = 40
$$

Write the division problem and solve it.

2

$20 \times 4 = 80$

$80 + 3 = 83$

Check your answer.

3

How many toy cars can we put together? 20

How many wheels will be left over? 3

Answer the questions.

Problem	Solve	Check
① Louie brings 93 wheels. How many toy cars can we put together? ______ How many wheels will be left over? ______		
② Louie brings 88 wheels. How many toy cars can we put together? ______ How many wheels will be left over? ______		

Home Note: Your child solves problems with the divisor 4.

Solve Problems with Fewer Steps

DIRECTIONS

Louie brings 93 wheels.

How many toy cars can we put together? ______

How many wheels will be left over? ______

1

$$\begin{array}{r} 3 \\ 20 \\ 4\overline{)93} \\ \underline{80} \\ 13 \\ \underline{12} \\ 1 \end{array} \rangle 23 \text{ R1}$$

$\textcircled{20} \times 4 = 80$

$\textcircled{3} \times 4 = 12$

Write the division problem and solve it.

2

$23 \times 4 = 92$

$92 + 1 = 93$

Check your answer.

3

How many toy cars can we put together? 23

How many wheels will be left over? 1

Answer the questions.

Problem	Solve	Check
(1) Louie brings 68 wheels. Each **tricycle** needs 3 wheels. How many tricycles can we put together? ______ How many wheels will be left over? ______		
(2) Louie brings 47 wheels. Each **bicycle** needs 2 wheels. How many bicycles can we put together? ______ How many wheels will be left over? ______		

Home Note: Your child uses fewer steps to solve division problems.

Solve Problems with Fewer Steps

DIRECTIONS

Louie brings 73 wheels.

How many tricycles can we put together? ______

How many wheels will be left over? ______

1

$$\begin{array}{r} 4 \\ 20 \\ 3\overline{)73} \\ \underline{60} \\ 13 \\ \underline{12} \\ 1 \end{array} \quad \begin{array}{l} \rangle\ 24 \text{ R1} \\ \\ \textcircled{20} \times 3 = 60 \\ \\ \textcircled{4} \times 3 = 12 \end{array}$$

Write the division problem and solve it.

2

$24 \times 3 = 72$

$72 + 1 = 73$

Check your answer.

3

How many tricycles can we put together? 24

How many wheels will be left over? 1

Answer the questions.

Problem	Solve	Check
(1) Louie brings 82 wheels. How many tricycles can we put together? ______ How many wheels will be left over? ______		
(2) Louie brings 58 wheels. How many bicycles can we put together? ______ How many wheels will be left over? ______		
(3) Louie brings 90 wheels. How many toy cars can we put together? ______ How many wheels will be left over? ______		

Home Note: Your child uses fewer steps to solve division problems.

Show What You Know

DIRECTIONS

➤ Solve each problem with division.

Problem	Solve	Check
(1) Sheila brings 86 wheels. How many tricycles can we put together? _____ How many wheels will be left over? _____		
(2) Sheila brings 54 wheels. How many toy cars can we put together? _____ How many wheels will be left over? _____		
(3) Sheila brings 35 wheels. How many bicycles can we put together? _____ How many wheels will be left over? _____		

Home Note: Your child solves division problems.

Problem	Solve	Check
(4) Sheila brings 70 wheels. How many tricycles can we put together? ______ How many wheels will be left over? ______		
(5) Sheila brings 96 wheels. How many toy cars can we put together? ______ How many wheels will be left over? ______		

Home Note: Your child solves division problems.

Target Zero

DIRECTIONS

10 20 30 40 ~~50~~ 60 70 80 90 100

1. **Number Rolled** — Roll 1: 4
   Roll the number cube. Write your number.
2. **Tens Number** — 50
   Choose a tens number. Cross it off the list.
3. **Equation** — $4 \times 50 = 200$
   Multiply. Write the equation.
4. **Score** — $1000 - 200 = 800$
   Subtract. Write your score.

10 20 30 40 50 60 70 80 90 100

Number Rolled	Tens Number	Equation	Score
Roll 1			
Roll 2			
Roll 3			
Roll 4			
Roll 5			
Roll 6			TOTAL

Home Note: Your child practices subtracting while playing a game.

Pennies Exchanged for Nickels

DIRECTIONS

There are 527 pennies.

How many nickels can they be exchanged for? ______

How many pennies are left over? ______

1

$$
\begin{array}{r}
5 \\
100 \\
5\overline{)527} \\
\underline{500} \\
27 \\
\underline{25} \\
2
\end{array}
\quad 105 \text{ R2}
$$

$(100) \times 5 = 500$

$(5) \times 5 = 25$

Write the division problem and solve it.

2

$105 \times 5 = 525$

$525 + 2 = 527$

Check your answer.

3

How many nickels can they be exchanged for? 105

How many pennies are left over? 2

Answer the questions.

Problem	Solve	Check
(1) There are 608 pennies. How many nickels can they be exchanged for? ______ How many pennies are left over? ______		

Home Note: Your child uses division to figure out how many nickels a number of pennies can be exchanged for.

Pennies Exchanged for Nickels

DIRECTIONS

There are 527 pennies.

How many nickels can they be exchanged for? ______

How many pennies will be left over? ______

1

$$\begin{array}{r} 5 \\ 100 \\ 5\overline{)527} \\ \underline{500} \\ 27 \\ \underline{25} \\ 2 \end{array} \quad 105 \text{ R2}$$

$(100) \times 5 = 500$

$(5) \times 5 = 25$

Write the division problem and solve it.

2

$105 \times 5 = 525$

$525 + 2 = 527$

Check your answer.

3

How many nickels can they be exchanged for? 105

How many pennies will be left over? 2

Answer the questions.

Problem	Solve	Check
(1) There are 615 pennies. How many nickels can they be exchanged for? ______ How many pennies will be left over? ______		
(2) There are 634 pennies. How many nickels can they be exchanged for? ______ How many pennies will be left over? ______		

Home Note: Your child uses division to figure out how many nickels a number of pennies can be exchanged for.

Pennies Exchanged for Nickels in Fewer Steps

DIRECTIONS

There are 734 pennies.

How many nickels can they be exchanged for?

_____

How many pennies will be left over? _____

1

$$\begin{array}{r} 6 \\ 40 \\ 100 \\ 5\overline{)734} \\ \underline{500} \\ 234 \\ \underline{200} \\ 34 \\ \underline{30} \\ 4 \end{array}$$

6 + 40 + 100 → 146 R4

(100) × 5 = 500

(40) × 5 = 200

(6) × 5 = 30

Write the division problem and solve it.

2

146 × 5 = 730

730 + 4 = 734

Check your answer.

3

How many nickels can they be exchanged for? 146

How many pennies will be left over? 4

Answer the questions.

Problem	Solve	Check
(1) There are 743 pennies. How many nickels can they be exchanged for? _____ How many pennies will be left over? _____		

Home Note: Your child uses fewer steps to solve penny problems.

Pennies Exchanged for Nickels in Fewer Steps

DIRECTIONS

There are 734 pennies.

How many nickels can they be exchanged for? ______

How many pennies will be left over? ______

1

$$\begin{array}{r} 6 \\ 40 \\ 100 \\ 5\overline{)734} \\ \underline{500} \\ 234 \\ \underline{200} \\ 34 \\ \underline{30} \\ 4 \end{array} \quad 146 \text{ R4}$$

$(100) \times 5 = 500$

$(40) \times 5 = 200$

$(6) \times 5 = 30$

Write the division problem and solve it.

2

$146 \times 5 = 730$

$730 + 4 = 734$

Check your answer.

3

How many nickels can they be exchanged for? 146

How many pennies will be left over? 4

Answer the questions.

Problem	Solve	Check
(1) There are 230 pennies. How many nickels can they be exchanged for? ______ How many pennies will be left over? ______		
(2) There are 828 pennies. How many nickels can they be exchanged for? ______ How many pennies will be left over? ______		

Home Note: Your child uses fewer steps to solve penny problems.

Roll and Divide

DIRECTIONS

➤ Write all the possible three-digit numbers.

______ ______ ______ ______ ______ ______

➤ Write the least possible dividend, solve the problem, and check.

$6\overline{)\quad\quad}$

Home Note: Your child divides a three-digit dividend by 6.

Roll and Divide

DIRECTIONS

1   

Roll the number cubes and record your numbers.

2 572 527 / 752 725 / 275 257

Write all the possible three-digit dividends.

3
$$\begin{array}{r} 5 \\ 40 \\ 6\overline{)275} \\ \underline{240} \\ 35 \\ \underline{30} \\ 5 \end{array} \quad 45 \text{ R5}$$

$\textcircled{40} \times 6 = 240$

$\textcircled{5} \times 6 = 30$

Choose and write a dividend. Then solve the problem.

4 $45 \times 6 = 270$

$270 + 5 = 275$

Check your answer.

Numbers Rolled	Possible Dividends	Solve	Check
①		$3\overline{)\quad}$	
②		$4\overline{)\quad}$	

Home Note: Your child divides three-digit numbers by one-digit numbers.

Roll and Divide

DIRECTIONS

1.   
Roll the number cubes and record your numbers.

2. 572 527
752 725
275 257
Write all the possible three-digit dividends.

3. $$\begin{array}{r} 5 \\ 40 \\ 6\overline{)275} \\ \underline{240} \\ 35 \\ \underline{30} \\ 5 \end{array}$$
5 + 40 → 45 R5
(40) × 6 = 240
(5) × 6 = 30
Choose and write a dividend. Then solve the problem.

4. $45 \times 6 = 270$
$270 + 5 = 275$
Check your answer.

Numbers Rolled	Possible Dividends	Solve	Check
(1)		$5\overline{)}$	
(2)		$6\overline{)}$	

Home Note: Your child divides three-digit numbers by one-digit numbers.

Divide and Check

DIRECTIONS

➤ Solve the problem and check your answer.

$$8\overline{)906}$$

Home Note: Your child divides a three-digit dividend by 8.

Roll and Divide

DIRECTIONS

1

Roll the number cubes and record your numbers.

2

840
804
480
408

Write all the possible three-digit dividends.

3

$$\begin{array}{r} 5 \\ 100 \\ 8\overline{)840} \\ \underline{800} \\ 40 \\ \underline{40} \\ 0 \end{array} \quad \Rightarrow 105$$

$\textcircled{100} \times 8 = 800$

$\textcircled{5} \times 8 = 40$

Choose and write a dividend. Then solve the problem.

4

$105 \times 8 = 840$

Check your answer.

Numbers Rolled	Possible Dividends	Solve	Check
1		$7\overline{)}$	
2		$9\overline{)}$	

Home Note: Your child divides three-digit numbers by one-digit numbers.

Roll and Divide

DIRECTIONS

1

Roll the number cubes and record your numbers.

2

844
448
484

Write all the possible three-digit dividends.

3

$$\begin{array}{r} 5 \\ 100 \\ 8\overline{)844} \\ \underline{800} \\ 44 \\ \underline{40} \\ 4 \end{array} \rightarrow 105\text{ R}4$$

$(100) \times 8 = 800$

$(5) \times 8 = 40$

Choose and write a dividend. Then solve the problem.

4

$105 \times 8 = 840$

$840 + 4 = 844$

Check your answer.

Numbers Rolled	Possible Dividends	Solve	Check
(1)		$8\overline{)\quad}$	
(2)		$9\overline{)\quad}$	

Home Note: Your child divides three-digit numbers by one-digit numbers.

Show What You Know

DIRECTIONS

➤ Solve each problem and check each answer.

Problem	Solve	Check
① There are 558 pennies. How many nickels can they be exchanged for? ______ How many pennies will be left over? ______		
② There are 610 pennies. How many nickels can they be exchanged for? ______ How many pennies will be left over? ______		
③ There are 267 pennies. How many nickels can they be exchanged for? ______ How many pennies will be left over? ______		

Home Note: Your child divides three-digit numbers by 5.

Show What You Know

DIRECTIONS

➤ Solve each problem and check each answer.

1. $4\overline{)956}$

2. $7\overline{)652}$

3. $8\overline{)452}$

4. $6\overline{)780}$

Home Note: Your child divides three-digit numbers by one-digit numbers.

Target Zero

DIRECTIONS

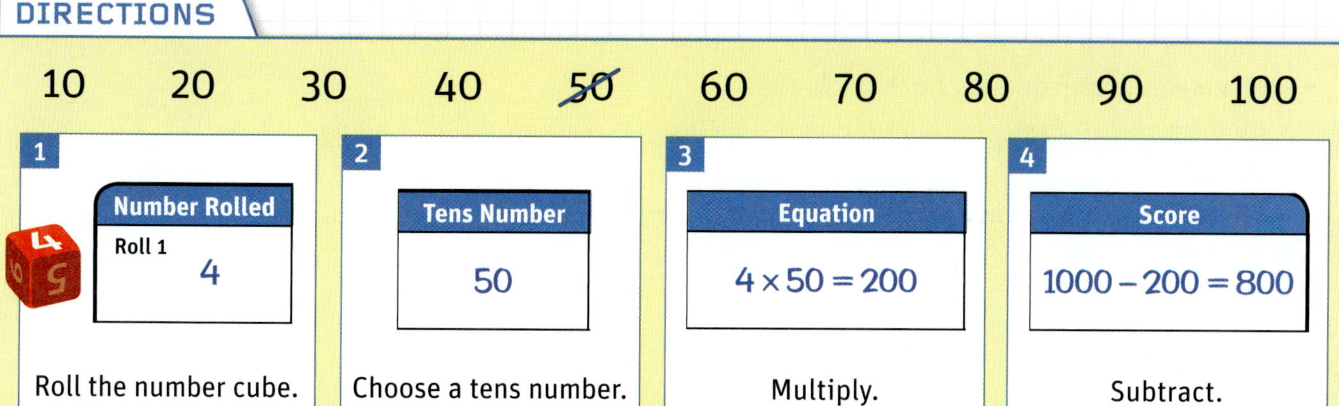

10 20 30 40 50 60 70 80 90 100

Number Rolled	Tens Number	Equation	Score
Roll 1			
Roll 2			
Roll 3			
Roll 4			
Roll 5			
Roll 6			TOTAL

Home Note: Your child practices subtracting by playing a game.

Dividing by 10

DIRECTIONS

➤ Solve each problem and check each answer.

(1)

$10\overline{)134}$

(2)

$10\overline{)732}$

Home Note: Your child divides three-digit numbers by 10.

Dividing by 10

DIRECTIONS

- Use the pattern to solve each problem.
- Choose two problems, do the division, and check the answer.

(1) 891 ÷ 10 = ______

(2) 128 ÷ 10 = ______

(3) 436 ÷ 10 = ______

(4) 944 ÷ 10 = ______

(5) 587 ÷ 10 = ______

(6) 352 ÷ 10 = ______

(7) 265 ÷ 10 = ______

(8) 116 ÷ 10 = ______

(9)	(10)
10)‾‾‾‾‾	10)‾‾‾‾‾

Home Note: Your child divides three-digit numbers by 10.

Rules for Target 25

HOW TO PLAY

What you need

- number cube (0, 2, 3, 4, 5, 6)
- number cube (1, 2, 4, 6, 7, 9)
- number cube (3, 5, 6, 7, 8, 9)
- *WorkSpace* page 53

➤ **A game is five turns for each player.**

➤ **Players add their remainders for the five turns.**

1

Player A rolls the number cubes.

2

567

Player A writes a three-digit dividend.

3

$567 \div 10 = 56$ (R7)

Player A divides the dividend by 10, writes the equation, and circles the remainder.

4

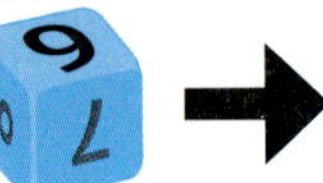

Player A hands the number cubes to Player B.

➤ **The winner is the player whose total is closer to 25—without going over—after five turns.**

Home Note: Your child practices dividing three-digit numbers by 10 by playing a game.

Target 25

DIRECTIONS

1  

Roll the number cubes.

2 268

Write a three-digit dividend with the three numbers.

3 $268 \div 10 = 26$ (R8)

Divide by 10. Circle the remainder.

Player A		Player B	
Numbers Rolled	**Division Equation**	**Numbers Rolled**	**Division Equation**
Roll 1		Roll 1	
Roll 2		Roll 2	
Roll 3		Roll 3	
Roll 4		Roll 4	
Roll 5		Roll 5	

Player A's total (add the remainders) ☐

Player B's total (add the remainders) ☐

Home Note: Your child practices dividing three-digit numbers by 10 by playing a game.

Target 25

DIRECTIONS

1   
Roll the number cubes.

2 268
Write a three-digit dividend with the three numbers.

3 $268 \div 10 = 26$ (R8)
Divide by 10. Circle the remainder.

Player A		Player B	
Numbers Rolled	**Division Equation**	**Numbers Rolled**	**Division Equation**
Roll 1		Roll 1	
Roll 2		Roll 2	
Roll 3		Roll 3	
Roll 4		Roll 4	
Roll 5		Roll 5	

Player A's total (add the remainders)

Player B's total (add the remainders)

Home Note: Your child practices dividing three-digit numbers by 10 by playing a game.

Divide and Check

DIRECTIONS

➤ **Solve the problem and check your answer.**

$30\overline{)489}$

Home Note: Your child divides a three-digit dividend by 30.

Divide and Check

DIRECTIONS

$50\overline{)788}$

$$\begin{array}{r} 5 \\ 10 \\ 50\overline{)788} \\ \underline{500} \\ 288 \\ \underline{250} \\ 38 \end{array} \quad 5 + 10 = 15 \text{ R}38$$

check: $15 \times 50 = 750$

$750 + 38 = 788$

Write the division problem, solve it, and check the answer.

Problem	Solve
1. $40\overline{)638}$	
2. $30\overline{)772}$	

Home Note: Your child divides three-digit numbers by multiples of 10.

Rules for Target 100

HOW TO PLAY

What you need

- number cube (0, 2, 3, 4, 5, 6)
- number cube (1, 2, 4, 6, 7, 9)
- number cube (3, 5, 6, 7, 8, 9)
- *WorkSpace* page 58

➤ **A game is five turns for each player.**

➤ **Players add their remainders for all five turns.**

1

567

Player A rolls the number cubes and writes a three-digit dividend.

2

10 20 30 40 50 60 70 80 90

$50\overline{)567}$

Player A chooses a divisor from the list.

3

$$\begin{array}{r} 1 \\ 10 \\ 50\overline{)567} \\ \underline{500} \\ 67 \\ \underline{50} \\ 17 \end{array} \quad \begin{array}{l} \to 11 \text{ (R17)} \\ \\ \\ 10 \times 50 = 500 \\ \\ 1 \times 50 = 50 \\ \\ \end{array}$$

Player A divides and circles the remainder.

4

Player A hands the number cubes to Player B.

➤ **The winner is the player whose total is closer to 100—without going over—after five turns.**

Home Note: Your child practices dividing three-digit numbers by multiples of 10 by playing a game.

Target 100

DIRECTIONS

10 20 30 40 50 60 70 80 90

1

Roll the number cubes.

2

735

Write a three-digit dividend.

3

$$70 \overline{)735} = 10 \text{ R}35$$

700 $10 \times 70 = 700$

35

check: $10 \times 70 = 700$

$700 + 35 = 735$

Choose a divisor from the list. Divide and check. Circle the remainder.

10 20 30 40 50 60 70 80 90

Numbers Rolled	Division	Numbers Rolled	Division
Roll 1		Roll 4	
Roll 2		Roll 5	
Roll 3		Your total (add your remainders)	
		Your partner's total	

Draw a star beside the winning score.

Home Note: Your child practices dividing three-digit numbers by multiples of 10 by playing a game.

Show What You Know

DIRECTIONS

➤ **Solve the problem and check each answer.**

1. $20\overline{)132}$

2. $30\overline{)367}$

Home Note: Your child divides three-digit numbers by multiples of 10.

(3)

$50\overline{)736}$

(4)

$40\overline{)880}$

DIRECTIONS

➤ Solve each problem.

(5) 657 ÷ 10 = ______

(6) 446 ÷ 10 = ______

(7) 198 ÷ 10 = ______

(8) 913 ÷ 10 = ______

(9) 329 ÷ 10 = ______

(10) 575 ÷ 10 = ______

Home Note: Your child divides three-digit numbers by multiples of 10.

Target 100

DIRECTIONS

10 20 30 40 50 60 70 80 90

1 Roll the number cubes.

2 735

Write a three-digit dividend.

3

$$70\overline{)735} = 10 \text{ (R35)}$$

$$735 - 700 = 35 \qquad 10 \times 70 = 700$$

check: $10 \times 70 = 700$
$700 + 35 = 735$

Choose a divisor from the list. Divide and check. Circle the remainder.

10 20 30 40 50 60 70 80 90

Numbers Rolled	Division	Numbers Rolled	Division
Roll 1		Roll 4	
Roll 2		Roll 5	
Roll 3		Your total (add your remainders)	
		Your partner's total	

Draw a star beside the winning score.

Home Note: Your child practices dividing three-digit numbers by multiples of 10 by playing a game.

Divide by 12

DIRECTIONS

➤ Solve each problem and check each answer.

1. $12\overline{)135}$

2. $12\overline{)284}$

3. $12\overline{)890}$

4. $12\overline{)533}$

Home Note: Your child divides three-digit numbers by 12.

Divide by 25

DIRECTIONS

➤ **Solve the problem and check your answer.**

$$25\overline{)284}$$

Home Note: Your child divides a three-digit number by 25.

Divide by 25

DIRECTIONS

➤ Solve each problem and check each answer.

1. $25\overline{)356}$

2. $25\overline{)301}$

3. $25\overline{)613}$

4. $25\overline{)825}$

Home Note: Your child divides three-digit numbers by 25.

Solve a Word Problem

DIRECTIONS

➤ Write and solve the division problem. Check your answer.

A factory makes jackets.
Each jacket has 16 buttons.
The factory has 520 buttons.

How many jackets can be made with these buttons?

Home Note: Your child solves a division word problem.

Solve a Word Problem

DIRECTIONS

➤ Write and solve each division problem. Check each answer.

Problem	Solve and Check
(1) A tile store has 606 tiles. They will be packed 25 to a box. How many boxes will be used? ________ How many tiles will be left over? ________	
(2) A machine packs crackers in stacks of 25. There are 888 crackers to pack. How many stacks will be packed? ________ How many crackers will be left over? ________	
(3) Lee puts apples in boxes of 15 apples. He picked 190 apples. How many boxes will he need? ________ How many apples will be left over? ________	

Home Note: Your child solves division word problems.

Write about Division

DIRECTIONS

➤ Tell about division with words, numbers, and pictures.

Home Note: Your child writes about division.

Show What You Know

DIRECTIONS

➤ Solve each problem and check each answer.

(1) $25\overline{)368}$	(2) $12\overline{)270}$
(3) $15\overline{)172}$	(4) $20\overline{)685}$
(5) $18\overline{)187}$	(6) $30\overline{)672}$

Home Note: Your child divides three-digit numbers by two-digit divisors.

DIRECTIONS

➤ Write and solve each division problem. Check each answer.

Problem	Solve and Check
(7) A garden store sells tulip bulbs in bags of 12. The store has 725 bulbs. How many bags will be filled? ______ How many bulbs will be left over? ______	
(8) A museum sells peanuts in bags of 25 peanuts each. The museum has 800 peanuts. How many bags can be filled? ______ How many peanuts will be left over? ______	

➤ Answer the question.

(9) In a long division problem, how do you know when you can stop dividing?

____

____

➤ Solve.

(10) $573 \div 10 =$ ______

Home Note: Your child solves division word problems.

Target 100

DIRECTIONS

10 20 30 40 50 60 70 80 90

1 Roll the number cubes.

2 735

Write a three-digit dividend.

3

$$\begin{array}{r} 10 \text{ (R35)} \\ 70\overline{)735} \\ \underline{700} \\ 35 \end{array} \qquad 10 \times 70 = 700$$

check: $10 \times 70 = 700$
$700 + 35 = 735$

Choose a divisor from the list. Divide and check. Circle the remainder.

10 20 30 40 50 60 70 80 90

Numbers Rolled	Division	Numbers Rolled	Division
Roll 1		**Roll 4**	
Roll 2		**Roll 5**	
Roll 3		**Your total (add your remainders)**	
		Your partner's total	

Draw a star beside the winning score.

Home Note: Your child practices dividing three-digit numbers by multiples of 10 by playing a game.

Math Vocabulary

DIRECTIONS

- Write new words and terms in the box.
- Write a definition, show an example, or draw a picture for each word or term in your list.

Home Note: Your child creates a math vocabulary word list.

Math Vocabulary

DIRECTIONS

- Write new words and terms in the box.
- Write a definition, show an example, or draw a picture for each word or term in your list.

Home Note: Your child creates a math vocabulary word list.

Target Zero

DIRECTIONS

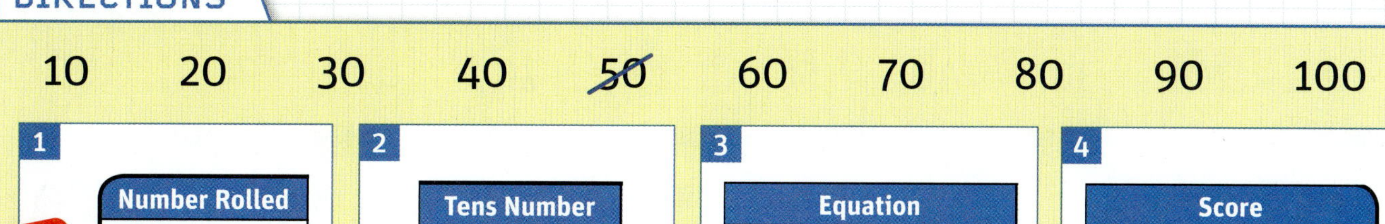

1. Number Rolled — Roll 1: 4

   Roll the number cube. Write your number.

2. Tens Number: 50

   Choose a tens number. Cross it off the list.

3. Equation: $4 \times 50 = 200$

   Multiply. Write the equation.

4. Score: $1000 - 200 = 800$

   Subtract. Write your score.

10 20 30 40 50 60 70 80 90 100

Number Rolled	Tens Number	Equation	Score
Roll 1			
Roll 2			
Roll 3			
Roll 4			
Roll 5			
Roll 6			TOTAL

Home Note: Your child practices subtracting while playing a game.

Target Zero

10 20 30 40 ~~50~~ 60 70 80 90 100

1. **Number Rolled** — Roll 1: 4
   Roll the number cube. Write your number.
2. **Tens Number** — 50
   Choose a tens number. Cross it off the list.
3. **Equation** — $4 \times 50 = 200$
   Multiply. Write the equation.
4. **Score** — $1000 - 200 = 800$
   Subtract. Write your score.

10 20 30 40 50 60 70 80 90 100

Number Rolled	Tens Number	Equation	Score
Roll 1			
Roll 2			
Roll 3			
Roll 4			
Roll 5			
Roll 6			TOTAL

Home Note: Your child practices subtracting while playing a game.

Target 100

DIRECTIONS

10 20 30 40 50 60 70 80 90

1

Roll the number cubes.

2

735

Write a three-digit dividend.

3

$$\begin{array}{r} 10 \ \text{(R35)} \\ 70\overline{)735} \\ \underline{700} \\ 35 \end{array} \qquad 10 \times 70 = 700$$

check: $10 \times 70 = 700$
$700 + 35 = 735$

Choose a divisor from the list. Divide and check. Circle the remainder.

10 20 30 40 50 60 70 80 90

Numbers Rolled	Division	Numbers Rolled	Division
Roll 1		Roll 4	
Roll 2		Roll 5	
Roll 3		Your total (add your remainders)	
		Your partner's total	

Draw a star beside the winning score.

Home Note: Your child practices dividing three-digit numbers by multiples of 10 by playing a game.

Target 100

DIRECTIONS

10 20 30 40 50 60 70 80 90

1

Roll the number cubes.

2

735

Write a three-digit dividend.

3

$$\begin{array}{r} 10 \text{ (R35)} \\ 70\overline{)735} \\ \underline{700} \\ 35 \end{array}$$

$10 \times 70 = 700$

check: $10 \times 70 = 700$
$700 + 35 = 735$

Choose a divisor from the list. Divide and check. Circle the remainder.

10 20 30 40 50 60 70 80 90

Numbers Rolled	Division	Numbers Rolled	Division
Roll 1		Roll 4	
Roll 2		Roll 5	
Roll 3		Your total (add your remainders)	
		Your partner's total	

Draw a star beside the winning score.

Home Note: Your child practices dividing three-digit numbers by multiples of 10 by playing a game.

Glossary

divide

When you split a number or separate a number of objects into equal groups you use the word *divide* to describe what you are doing. For example if you separate 12 cookies into 3 equal groups (written like this: $12 \div 3$), you divide 12 by 3.

divided by

We read $12 \div 3 = 4$ this way: *12 divided by 3 is equal to 4*. The symbol $\div$ means *divided by.*

dividend

The number being divided into equal groups is the *dividend*. In the equation $20 \div 5 = 4$, 20 is the *dividend*.

divisible

When you get a zero remainder, you can say that the *dividend* is *divisible* by the *divisor*. For example, 20 is divisible by 5 because the quotient is 4 and the remainder is zero. 23 is not divisible by 5 because there is a remainder of 3 ($23 \div 5 = 4$ R3).

division

Division is the word for what we do when we divide.

division equation

A *division equation* is a number sentence that has two sides separated by an equal sign. Both sides have the same value and there is a division on one or both sides. Examples of *division equations* are $24 \div 6 = 4$ and $5 = 15 \div 3$.

divisor

The number you are dividing by is called the *divisor*. In the equation $12 \div 3 = 4$, the 3 is the *divisor*.

We can also write the division as $3\overline{)12}$ with 4 above, and $\frac{12}{3} = 4$ where 3 is the divisor. The divisor 3 tells us that we want to know how many groups of 3 are in 12.

equal groups

Equal groups means each group has the same amount. For example, if there are three circles and each circle has 2 stars, then there are three equal groups of two stars.

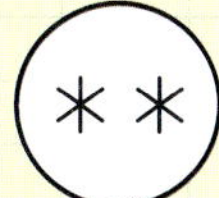
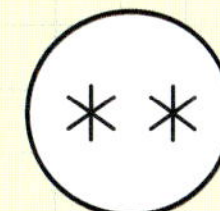
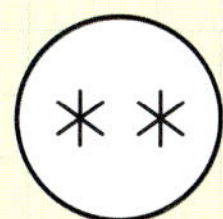

equation

An *equation* is a number sentence that uses an equal sign to show that two amounts have the same value. For example $12 \div 3 = 4$ is an *equation*.

Glossary

grouping problem

A problem is a *grouping problem* when there are a number of things being put in equal groups and you want to figure out how many groups there are. We can use division to solve a grouping problem.

An example of a *grouping problem* is:

There are 24 students. (number to begin with)

Each relay team will have 6 students. (equal groups)

How many relay teams will they make? (number of groups)

$24 \div 6 = 4$, so there are 4 teams.

multiplication

When you write $2 \times 3 = $ ____, you are asking, *How many in all when there are 2 equal groups of 3?* We use the symbol × to show multiplication. *Multiplication* is related to division. To solve $28 \div 4 = $ ____, we say, *What number times 4 equals 28?* (____ $\times 4 = 28$) Since $7 \times 4 = 28$, the answer to the division problem is 7. ($28 \div 4 = 7$)

quotient

A *quotient* is the answer to the question, How many equal groups of ____ are in ____? For example, *How many groups of 2 are in 25* or *What is 25 divided by 2?* The answer is 12. There are 12 groups of 2 in 25 so 12 is the *quotient*.

remainder

When we divide a number by another number, we are finding the number of equal groups. Sometimes there are leftovers because there aren't enough to make another group.

For example, $8 \div 3$ means *How many equal groups of 3 are in 8?*

Dividing 8 into groups of 3 gives us 2 groups of 3 with 2 left over. The 2 is the *remainder*.

We write it this way: $8 \div 3 = 2$ R2

sharing problem

A problem is a *sharing problem* when there are a number of things being shared equally and you want to find out how many will be in each group.

An example of a *sharing problem* is:

There are 12 marbles. (number to begin with)

3 friends are going to share them. (number who will share)

How many marbles will each one get? (how many in each group)

We write it this way: $12 \div 3 = $ ____.
Each friend will get 4 marbles.

symbols

You use *symbols* in mathematics to name numbers (12, 308, $\frac{1}{2}$), operations (+, −, ×, ÷), and relationships between numbers (=, >, <).

symbols for division

÷ means *is divided by*

$\frac{12}{3}$ The fraction bar is a division symbol. This means 12 divided by 3.

$3\overline{)12}$ The partial box around the 12 tells us that 12 is to be divided by 3. The quotient is written on the line above the 12.

$\begin{array}{r} 4 \\ 3\overline{)12} \end{array}$ $\qquad$ $\begin{array}{r} \text{quotient} \\ \text{divisor}\overline{)\text{dividend}} \end{array}$